THE LITTLE BOOK
OF

THE LITTLE BOOK
OF
Despair

Michael Powell

Michael O'Mara Humour

First published in Great Britain in 2001 by
Michael O'Mara Books Limited
9 Lion Yard, Tremadoc Road
London SW4 7NQ

A CIP catalogue record for this book is available
from the British Library

ISBN 1-85479-818-9

1 3 5 7 9 10 8 6 4 2

Designed and typeset by Martin Bristow

Printed in Australia by McPherson's Printing Group

Contents

Introduction

YOU HAVE TRIED BOOKS urging you to be calm. They made you almost apopleptic, with their vague panaceas and infuriating niceness. So you turned to affirmations (remember them?), but found that leaving notes for yourself in the fridge saying 'Yes! You *are* a truly worthwhile person' was not only self-deceiving, but deeply embarrassing as well.

'Aha!' you thought, 'aromatherapy is the one for me.' But the smell made you feel ill. Crystals? Like a small chunk of amethyst is going to make you rich, successful and happy? Meditation taught you only one useful trick, namely that closing your eyes, extending your arms and humming 'Om-m-m-m-m!' is a good way of getting rid of people you don't want to talk to in double-quick time. Yoga? You *like* having back problems?

And so on, through dream-interpretation, relationship theory, instant-happiness guides and self-improvement books, none of which were any use unless you happened to have a short leg on a table. Somehow, though, the nagging question wouldn't go away. Somewhere, there had to be an answer to all those questions about the meaning of existence and the true route to happiness and inner fulfilment.

There *is* an answer, and this book provides it: despair. After all, as Oscar Wilde partly remarked, 'We are all of us in the gutter.' Full stop. With *The Little Book of Despair*, you can learn to look at life not just with a jaundiced eye, but with one that is positively teeming with the nastier forms of hepatitis as well. Despair provides the antidote to fatuous optimism, misguided self-belief, and pointless quests for inner calm; as for sorting out relationships, why bet on non-starters? Thus fortified by the hundreds of helpful tips in this book, you will quickly see that there is now only one way to look.

Upwards.

Life – A Half Empty Glass?

Life is perhaps most wisely regarded as a bad dream between two awakenings, and every day is a life in miniature.
EUGENE O'NEILL

❋

Count your blessings every day. Then when someone breaks into your house, you'll know how many of your blessings are missing.

❋

Two wrongs are just the start.

❋

If God meant us to be happy . . .
we'd be happy.

Despair is when you wake up screaming and you realize that you haven't fallen asleep yet.

✳

Remember it takes both sunshine and rain to make a rainbow. Pouring petrol into a dirty puddle also works.

✳

All the world's a stage – shame your part is a walk-on.

✳

A vacuum is a hell of a lot better than some of the stuff that nature replaces it with.

TENNESSEE WILLIAMS

When everything comes your way,
you're in the wrong lane.

✳

Sometimes you just gotta go with the flow.
Especially when you're drowning.

✳

If you don't ask, you don't get – but
ninety-nine times out of a hundred you ask
and still get bugger all.

✳

Life is like a love-bite. It feels great at first,
then it gets big and ugly, and then slowly
fades away.

You're not completely useless. Your life can
be used as a bad example to others.

✳

Don't allow your mind to wander.
It's too small to be allowed out on its own.

✳

Live every day like your last.
One day you'll be right.

✳

Some of us learn by other people's mistakes –
the rest of us have to be the other people.

✳

There's no place like there.

Always aim high if you don't want to
piss on your shoes.

✳

Just remember . . . if the world didn't suck,
we'd all fall off.

✳

We are born naked, wet, and hungry.
Then things get worse.

✳

Don't kick a man when he's down unless
you're certain he won't get up.

✳

If it's good, they discontinue it.

Due to recent cutbacks, the light at the end of the tunnel has been turned off.

✳

If life deals you lemons, why not go kill someone with them?

✳

Behind every cloud is a blue sky. Pity there's always a sodding cloud in front of it.

✳

Every time a bell rings, an angel gets his wings bitten off.

✳

Happiness is a belt-fed weapon.

Patience is a minor form of despair,
disguised as a virtue.

✳

Consciousness:
that irritating time between naps.

✳

Take control of your life. Buy a gun today!

✳

Every door that closes in your life,
was once a door that opened earlier
when another door closed.

✳

Do hernias have people?

Celebrate that thorns have roses.
Then remember that's a load of bollocks.
Roses have thorns. Deal with it.

✳

Today stretches ahead of you waiting
to be sculpted. You are the sculptor.
You are the tool.
Repeat three times: I am a great big tool.

✳

The meek just say 'Sod it!'
They're all tooled up and ready to kick arse.

✳

You've had fun before.
But not in this life.

Why do people say that life is filled with disappointments, when actually it's just one big disappointment?

✳

Abandon the search for truth – settle on a good fantasy.

✳

Happiness is merely the remission of pain.

✳

If you keep an open mind, eventually your brains will fall out.

✳

If you went to college to become a wit, you only got halfway through.

You can't control everything around you – so don't try, unless you are holding an automatic weapon.

✳

A grudge is too heavy a load for anyone to carry. Use a wheelbarrow.

✳

It is your frame of mind that determines what sort of day you are going to have. When you wake up in the morning, look in the mirror and say: 'Today I will see something special in this lousy pointless vacuum that is my existence.'

✳

Same shit, different day.

Life is too short to get bitter.
Get even instead.

✳

Live each day as if your life has just begun.
Cry a lot and piss yourself every two hours.

✳

How come boring people never lose
their voices?

✳

Aspire to principles, behave with virtue,
abide by benevolence, and cry yourself to
sleep every night.

✳

A life lived . . . is nearly over.

Every day you learn something
that someone else already knew.

✳

If God gives you lemons, form a rival
global religion around them.

✳

If you can't say something nice,
say nothing at all. Just sit in the corner
and sneer at everyone.

✳

Screw up your life,
you've screwed everything else up.

✳

If triangles had a God, He'd have three sides.

A wise old owl sat on an oak.
The more he learned, the less he spoke.
The less he spoke, the more he heard.
That dumb old bastard looked absurd.

✳

Life's a bitch, and then she has puppies.

✳

Happiness is best when you're enjoying the
misery of another.

✳

Whenever a friend succeeds, a little
something in me dies.
GORE VIDAL

Cheer up! Things are getting worse
at a slower rate.

✳

Always forgive your enemies. They hate that!

✳

Reach for the stars and you'll end up
in a cold, dark vacuum.

✳

The number of people watching you is
directly proportional to the stupidity
of your action.

✳

When people are free to do as they please,
they usually imitate each other.

You Know Life Sucks When . . .

You wake up face down on the pavement.

✳

You call the Samaritans
and they put you on hold.

✳

You wake up and your waterbed has broken.
Then you remember you don't have a
waterbed.

Your boss tells you not to bother removing your coat.

✳

You put your bra on backwards and it fits better.

All Work and No Play . . .

I'm already disturbed.
Please don't come in.

✳

Thought for Monday:
Next Monday is just seven days away.

✳

The world is divided into two types of
people: those who do stuff and those who
take all the credit.

✳

Do you remember when you looked forward
to getting the salary you can't live on today?

Knowledge is power.
Power corrupts.
Corruption is a crime.
Crime doesn't pay.
So if you keep studying,
you'll end up broke!

✳

Human beings were created by water
to transport it uphill.

✳

If you're not the lead dog, you'll always be
looking up someone else's arse.

By working hard eight hours a day
you may eventually get to be a boss
and work fourteen hours a day.

✳

If at first you don't succeed,
you're a lousy failure.

✳

If everything seems to be going well,
you have overlooked something.

✳

Don't be so humble,
you're not that great.

It's hard to make a comeback
when you haven't been anywhere.

✳

Do you feel like a one-legged man
in an arse-kicking contest?

✳

Some people are going to leave a mark
on this world, but you will probably leave
a stain.

✳

A pat on the back is only a few inches
from a kick in the butt.

Monday is an awful way to spend
one-seventh of your life.

✳

The dumber people think you are,
the more surprised they're going to be
when you kill them.

✳

See every failure as a wonderful opportunity
for others to take the piss out of you.

✳

You have the power to make positive choices
in your life. Today, you can either go to work
in a dead-end job for a boss you hate, or stay
in bed with a bottle of vodka and watch TV.

It is not winning that is important – it's how many lives you can ruin before you lose.

✳

When opportunity knocks on your door, will you be there to open it? Quit your job and stay at home waiting for opportunity to knock.

✳

The way to develop self-confidence is to do in the thing you fear.

✳

People seldom walk over you until you lie down. But standing up makes it easier for them to kick you in the nuts.

Don't be afraid to fail. If you fail once,
you'll be better at failing next time.

✳

Today, do not judge another,
think negatively, or be envious . . .
until you get to work.

✳

The beatings will continue
until morale improves.

✳

Your incompetence is an inspiration
to morons everywhere.

What you lack in intelligence, you more
than make up for in stupidity.

✻

Fools rush in where fools have been before.

✻

You must have learned from others' mistakes.
You haven't had the time to think all those
up yourself.

✻

Any time you think you have influence,
try ordering around someone else's dog.

If you can't learn to do it well,
learn to enjoy doing it badly.

✳

Law of Blame:
Whatever it is that hits the fan
will not be evenly distributed.

✳

Hang in there!
Retirement is only thirty years away!

Why Prison Is Better than Work

In prison you spend the day
in an 8-by-10-foot cell.
**At work you spend the day
in a 6-by-10-foot cubicle.**

❋

In prison you get three free meals a day.
**At work you only get a break for one meal
which you have to pay for.**

In prison you get time off for good behaviour.
**At work you get rewarded for good
behaviour with more work.**

✳

In prison a guard locks and unlocks
all the doors for you.
**At work you have to carry a security card
and unlock and open all the doors yourself.**

✳

In prison you can watch TV and play games.
**At work you get sacked for watching TV
and playing games.**

In prison you get your own toilet.
At work you share a toilet with fifty other people.

❋

In prison your family and friends can visit.
At work you can't even speak to your family and friends.

❋

In prison all expenses are paid by taxpayers, usually with no work required.
At work you pay all the expenses to go to work and taxes are taken from your salary to pay for prisoners.

In prison you spend most of your life
looking through bars from the inside
wanting to get out.
**At work you spend most of your time
wanting to get out and go inside bars.**

✳

In prison there are wardens
who are often sadistic.
At work they are called managers.

The Laws of Work

Important letters that contain no errors
will develop errors in the mail.

✳

There will always be beer cans rolling
on the floor of your car when the boss asks
for a ride home from the office.

✳

After any salary rise, you will have
less money at the end of the month
than you did before.

If it wasn't for the last minute,
nothing would get done.

✳

When you don't know what to do,
walk fast and look worried.

✳

The last person that quit or was fired
will be held responsible for everything
that goes wrong.

An Exercise
in Meaningful
Communication

The six most important words:
I know that you are wrong.

✳

The five most important words:
You did a lousy job.

✳

The four most important words:
What were you thinking?

The three most important words:
Why don't you . . .

✳

The two most important words:
Let me . . .

✳

The most important word:
No.

Looking for Love – Like Nailing Jelly to a Goat

There is no such thing as society.
MARGARET THATCHER

✳

Kissing is just a way of getting two people so
close together that they can't see anything
wrong with each other.

✳

Always remember you're unique,
just like everyone else.

✳

The less you cry,
the more you have to pee.

So, you turned out to be one of those people
your parents warned you about.

❋

There are easier things than meeting a good
person – like nailing jelly to a goat.

❋

If you think there is good in everybody,
you haven't met everybody.

❋

Try to imagine yourself with a personality.

❋

Next year, you'll look back on today
and start crying all over again.

The people you care most about in life are
taken from you too soon. And all the less
important ones never go away.

✳

You've got to have style
before someone can cramp it.

✳

Be yourself.
No one else wants the job.

✳

A friend is one who knows all about you
and won't go away. So is a stalker.

True friends don't stab you in the back.
They shoot you – it's more humane.

✳

Friends are just people whose telephone
numbers we haven't lost yet.

✳

If we are put on this earth to help others,
what are the others here for?

✳

Just for today be vulnerable with someone
you trust. Ask a friend to kick you in
the bollocks.

You may not think that you don't have
an enemy in the world, but all your friends
hate you.

✳

Of all the people in the world,
you're one of them.

✳

Sure, there are plenty of other fish in the sea.
But who wants to shag a fish?

✳

If you love something, turn it loose.
If it doesn't come back, kill it!

You can't make someone love you, you can only stalk them and hope they panic.

✳

It doesn't matter how passionate a relationship is at first. The passion soon disappears and there had better be lots of money to take its place.

✳

Reach for the stars – and try to cut off some of their clothing as a souvenir. Then stalk them.

Falling doesn't make you a failure.
Not getting laid makes you a failure.
And if you keep falling over and can't get
laid, you're a complete failure.

❋

When you are feeling down, give a little
whistle. It won't make you feel better,
but at least it will piss everybody else off.

❋

The climate of your heart will forecast the
weather of your day. But weather forecasts
are usually wrong.

The average person doesn't give a shit
about the average person.

✳

Everyone you meet doesn't know something
that you do know. Find out what it is and
exploit their weakness.

✳

Two is a couple, three is a crowd, four is two
couples, five is a couple and a crowd, six is
either three couples or two crowds, seven
is two couples and a crowd, eight is four
couples, nine is three crowds and ten
is either five couples or two crowds
and two couples . . .

People are scum. You have to realize that,
and work with it.

✳

It doesn't *take* all kinds – we just *have*
all kinds.

✳

Opposites attract. So be miserable and you'll
be surrounded by bright and cheerful people.

✳

Free yourself of all prejudices. Hate everyone
equally.

Your heart can see what is invisible
to your eye – your ribcage.

❋

If you keep a fire in your heart, you'd better
keep a bucket of water under your bed.

❋

Eat some ice cream and move on.

Looks Aren't Everything . . .

Spring makes everything look filthy.
KATHERINE WHITEHORN

✳

Whatever kind of look you were going for –
you failed.

✳

A smiling face is always beautiful,
unless the teeth are crooked.

✳

You have a winning smile.
Shame the rest of you is such a loser.

God must really love ugly people because he created so many of them. Although nothing worthwhile is ever achieved without making lots of rejects first.

✳

Love nature, despite what it did to you.

✳

If a thing of beauty is a joy for ever, why does ugly seem to last so much longer?

✳

If you entered an ugly contest, they'd say 'Sorry, no professionals.'

Each person's life is a portrait of themselves.
Shame you chose finger painting.

✳

God made you as ugly as he possibly could,
then he must have beaten you in the face
with a claw hammer.

✳

You have everything you had twenty years
ago – except now it's all lower.

✳

Instead of waiting for someone to bring you
flowers, why not pick them from your
neighbour's garden?

The only disability in life is a bad attitude.
But a bad attitude and acne is worse.

✳

Remember that there is always someone,
somewhere in the world, who is richer,
younger and better-looking than you.

As Long as You've Got Your Health . . .

Some mornings, it's just not worth chewing through the leather straps.
EMO PHILLIPS

✳

Life is like haemorrhoids – sometimes even the tiniest crap can really hurt.

✳

Start off every day with a smile and get it over with.

You know you're getting old when you stoop to tie your shoes and wonder what else you can do while you're down there.

✳

Early to bed, early to rise, makes a man healthy, wealthy and boring.

✳

Avoid health foods. You need all the preservatives you can get.

✳

If we are what we eat – you're cheap, fast, and easy.

Health is merely the slowest possible rate
at which you can die.

✳

The gene pool could use a little chlorine.

✳

All the good ones, no matter what they are,
are taken.

✳

Life is a sexually transmitted disease
for which there is no cure.

✳

Life is one long process of getting tired.
SAMUEL BUTLER

All people smile in the same language –
regardless of whether they shave their
underarm hair.

✳

Most smiles are started by another smile.
Or someone falling over.

✳

The journey of a thousand miles starts with a
single step. And ends with joint problems.

✳

If God wanted you to touch your toes,
he would have put them on your knees.

Rehab is for quitters.

✳

Reality is a crutch for people who can't
handle drugs.

✳

You need to bang your head against a wall for
eight hours to burn off the calories in the
quarter-pounder you've just eaten.

✳

You are what you don't throw up.

✳

There is no such thing as sleep deprivation,
only caffeine deficiency.

From the age of thirty, humans gradually
begin to shrink in size.

✳

By age sixty, most people have lost half of
their taste buds.

✳

Turn your life around. Don't be depressed
and miserable. Instead, try being miserable
and depressed.

✳

If ignorance is bliss,
you must be orgasmic.

When you feel depressed, pamper yourself with an aromatherapy bath. Light some candles and let the restless babble of other people's criticism fade from your mind as you enjoy the feeling of the water gently caressing you. Let go. Exhale. Then allow your whole body to sink under the water. Breathe in. Now how do you feel?

Signs You Are Stressed

You can get a big buzz
just by turning your head.

✳

You develop the ability to count
the number of times a humming bird
flaps its wings.

✳

To save time, you stop adding water
to your coffee.

✳

You believe that if you think hard enough,
you can fly.

Your heart beats in seven-eighths time.

✳

It appears that people are speaking to you in hexadecimal.

✳

Indigestion tablets become your only source of nutrition.

✳

You have an irresistible desire to bite the noses of those around you.

✳

Your mobile phone is set to 'Stun'.

You listen to relaxation tapes
on fast forward.

✳

Your 'to do' list is so big
you have to tie the pages together
with pink ribbon.

✳

Your wife and your girlfriend
are in the same maternity ward.

Death and Taxes

In the midst of life we are in death.
The Book of Common Prayer

✳

In dog years, you died a decade ago.

✳

You are dying a slow, horrible, lingering life.

✳

When long you stare at the abyss,
You'll soon be dying for a piss.

Life is just something to do
when you can't get to sleep.

✳

Eat right.
Stay fit.
Die anyway.

✳

Life can little more supply,
than just to look about us and to die.
ALEXANDER POPE

✳

The more you complain,
the longer God lets you live.

Life is not lost by dying; life is lost
minute by minute, day by dragging day,
in all the thousand small uncaring ways.
STEPHEN VINCENT BENÉT

❊

He who dies last wins.

Reasons to Be Cheerful?

The first half of our lives is ruined by our parents, and the second half by our children.
CLARENCE DARROW

✳

Life is a horizontal fall.
JEAN COCTEAU

✳

What's the point in prolonging the inevitable? We're all just a stitch away from here to there.
WHEEZY THE PENGUIN
Toy Story 2

The world itself is but a large prison,
out of which some are daily led to execution.
SIR WALTER RALEGH

❋

Most of the time I don't have much fun.
The rest of the time I don't have any fun
at all.
WOODY ALLEN

❋

The wailing of the newborn infant
is mingled with the dirge for the dead.
LUCRETIUS

We should weep for men at their birth,
not at their death.
BARON DE MONTESQUIEU

✳

Millions long for immortality who do not
know what to do with themselves
on a rainy Sunday afternoon.
SUSAN ERTZ

✳

We should forgive our enemies,
but only after they have been hanged first.
HEINRICH HEINE

There is a thin line between genius and insanity. I have erased this line.
OSCAR LEVANT

✳

The basic fact about human existence is not that it is a tragedy, but that it is a bore.
H. L. MENCKEN

✳

We are born crying, live complaining, and die disappointed.
THOMAS FULLER

✳

There is no new thing under the sun.
ECCLESIASTES 1:9

My pessimism goes to the point of suspecting
the sincerity of pessimists.
JEAN ROSTAND

❃

Cheer up! The worst is yet to come!
PHILANDER JOHNSON

❃

The object of life is not to be on the side of
the majority, but to escape finding oneself
in the ranks of the insane.
MARCUS AURELIUS

❃

Maybe this world is another planet's Hell.
ALDOUS HUXLEY

All animals except man know that the
ultimate of life is to enjoy it.
SAMUEL BUTLER

✳

Any idiot can face a crisis; it is this
day-to-day living that wears you out.
ANTON CHEKHOV

✳

What sane person could live in this world
and not be crazy?
URSULA LEGUIN

✳

We come and go just like ripples in a stream.
JOHN V. POLITIS

Search for meaning, eat, sleep.
Search for meaning, eat, sleep.
Die, search for meaning,
search for meaning,
search for meaning.
DOUG HORTON

✳

Life is a rollercoaster.
Try to eat a light lunch.
DAVID A. SCHMALTZ

✳

Life is a tale told by an idiot,
full of sound and fury,
signifying nothing.
WILLIAM SHAKESPEARE
Macbeth, V.v.

[75]

Life is but a dream,
a grotesque and foolish dream.
Mark Twain

✳

God is a comedian playing to an audience
too afraid to laugh.
Voltaire

✳

If at first you don't succeed,
try, and try again. Then give up.
There's no sense in being a damned fool
about it.
W. C. Fields

If at first you don't succeed,
failure may be your style.
QUENTIN CRISP

❋

Success is like a fart – only your own
smells nice.
JAMES P. HOGAN

❋

The more you wrestle with a turd,
the more shit gets on you.
SHELLY HORTON

❋

If there is a wrong way to do something,
then someone will do it.
EDWARD A. MURPHY, JR.

Happiness is nothing more than
good health and a bad memory.
ALBERT SCHWEITZER

✳

Passionate hatred can give meaning
and purpose to an empty life.
ERIC HOFFER

✳

Don't wait for the last judgment.
It happens every day.
ALBERT CAMUS

Lies, Damned Lies and Statistics

13 people a year are killed by vending machines falling on them.

✳

By 65 years old, you will have have watched more than nine years of television.

✳

10% of life is what happens to you and the other 90% is who you have sex with.

✳

107 incorrect medical procedures will be performed by the end of today.

Be kind to others. They outnumber you 5.9 billion to one.

✳

A standard grave is 7'8" x 3'2" x 6'.

✳

150 million blood cells in your body have died while you were reading this sentence.

✳

It takes 27 minutes of gardening to burn 100 calories.

✳

Every hour there are 9,700 extra people on the Earth. Go back to bed and ponder your own insignificance.

The first 90% of a project takes 90% of
the time, the last 10% takes the other 90%
of the time.

✳

It takes 76 muscles to frown and 6 to smile.
So be miserable and burn more calories.

✳

If the odds are a million to one against
something bad occurring, chances are
50:50 it will.

✳

A computer can make as many mistakes
in 2 seconds as 20 men working
for 20 years.

The Love of Money Is the Root of All Evil

You started out with nothing and still have
most of it left.

✳

The real reason you can't take it with you
when you go is that it's usually gone already.

✳

Cultivate the company of those who are
seeking the truth. They can be more easily
persuaded to part with their money.

✳

A penny saved is just another damn thing
to choke on.

If you ever see a poor man giving away everything he owns to help a person in need, pause for a moment to remind yourself of one of life's greatest lessons: it doesn't matter how poor a person is, he can still be a gullible prat.

✳

No life is so hard that you can't make it easier by stealing.

✳

A penny saved is not even enough to take a leak with any more.

✳

Forget yesterday, live for today, and pay it back in seventy-two monthly instalments.

It is by giving that we get rid of stuff we don't
want any more.

✳

Patronize someone less fortunate than
yourself today.

✳

All the poor people in the world would lack
nothing if there weren't so many of them.

✳

Help a man when he is in trouble and he will
remember you the next time he is in trouble.

✳

All the money in the world
cannot make up for what you don't have.

Do what you love and the money will come –
after you're dead.

✳

It is easier for a camel to pass through
the eye of a needle if it's been through
a blender first.

✳

The Golden Rule:
whoever has the gold makes the rules.

Random Negative-Thought Generator

Don't just be depressed, be the cause of depression in others as well, with the Random Negative-Thought Generator. Pick one of the following statements at random to share with your family, friends and colleagues.

✳

There's always a fresh problem around the next corner.

✳

Good times end quicker than bad times.

Pessimists see problems and optimists see challenges. But they're still problems.

✳

Wherever you go you meet stupid people.

✳

It's the stupid people who prevent us from doing what we want.

✳

Whenever luck is involved, it's usually bad.

✳

Your computer will never be fast enough.

Don't you wish you were paid to complain?

✳

It doesn't matter because we all die anyway.

✳

Looks like it's going to rain again today.

✳

Looks like we're going to bomb Iraq again
today.

✳

The ugly people are taking over the planet.

✳

Is it time to go home yet?

Did you know that in several million years time the sun will grow into a red giant and swallow the earth?

❋

Nothing is going to change.

❋

I feel really tired today, don't you?

❋

Have you ever tried to criticize someone and ended up making things worse?

❋

When you feel like your life is going down the toilet, try closing the lid.
Laugh at your problems; everybody else does.

Laugh at your problems; everybody else does.

✳

Losers of the world unite. On second thoughts, why bother? Nobody will pay any attention to a bunch of losers.

✳

If you were in a biggest-loser competition you'd win easily . . . unless there was a prize.

✳

You may be a loser, but at least it hasn't gone unnoticed.

It is easy for others to criticize you for feeling paranoid. Remember that if everybody hated them, they'd be paranoid too.

✳

Be a window into the abyss.
Divine Substance is everywhere present, but Doggy Substance is everywhere present more.

✳

If you want to shovel shit, buy a large shovel and stand in the street with a big sign on your chest which says 'SHIT SHOVELLER FOR HIRE'. That usually works.

Twenty-four hours in a day. Twenty-four beers in a case. Coincidence?

✳

Just because you've been wiping your arse for twenty years, it doesn't mean you've been doing it right.

A Cautionary Tale

Once upon a time, there was a lazy little
sparrow who couldn't be bothered to fly
south for the winter. However, once the
weather turned bitterly cold, the sparrow
realized he had made a big mistake. So he
flew off and headed south. After a while,
ice began to form on his wings and he fell
to earth in a barnyard, almost frozen.
A cow passed by and crapped on this little
bird and the sparrow thought it was the end,
but the dung warmed him and defrosted
his tiny wings. Warm and happy the little
sparrow opened his beak wide and started to
sing. Just then, a large cat wandered by and,
hearing the chirping, investigated the
sounds. As Old Tom cleared away the

manure, he found the chirping bird and
promptly gobbled him up.

❋

There are three morals to this story:

Everyone who shits on you is not necessarily
your enemy.

Everyone who gets you out of the shit is not
necessarily your friend.

If you are warm and happy in a pile of shit,
keep your mouth shut.

Michael O'Mara Humour

*Now you can order other little books directly
from Michael O'Mara Books.*

All at £1.99 each including postage (UK only)

The Little Book of Farting ISBN 1-85479-445-0
The Little Book of Stupid Men ISBN 1-85479-454-X
The Little Toilet Book ISBN 1-85479-456-6
The Little Book of Venom ISBN 1-85479-446-9
The Little Book of Pants ISBN 1-85479-477-9
The Little Book of Pants 2 ISBN 1-85479-557-0
The Little Book of Bums ISBN 1-85479-561-9
The Little Book of Revenge ISBN 1-85479-562-7
The Little Book of Voodoo ISBN 1-85479-560-0
The Little Book of Blondes ISBN 1-85479-558-9
The Little Book of Magical Love Spells ISBN 1-85479-559-7
WAN2TLK? ltle bk of txt msgs ISBN 1-85479-678-X
RUUP4IT? ltle bk of txt d8s ISBN 1-85479-892-8
LUVTLK: ltle bk of luv txt ISBN 1-85479-890-1
IH8U: ltle bk of txt abuse ISBN 1-85479-832-4
URGr8! ltle bk of pwr txt ISBN 1-85479-817-0
ltle bk of pics & tones ISBN 1-85479-563-5

The Little Book of Cockney Rhyming Slang ISBN 1-85479-825-1

The Little Book of Gay Gags ISBN 1-85479-590-2

The Little Book of Irish Grannies' Remedies ISBN 1-85479-828-6

The Little Book of Scottish Grannies' Remedies ISBN 1-85479-829-4

The Little Book of Irish Wit and Wisdom ISBN 1-85479-827-8

The Little Book of Scottish Wit and Wisdom ISBN 1-85479-826-X

The Little Book of the SAS ISBN 1-85479-887-1

101 Really Unpleasant Things About Men ISBN 1-85479-881-2

Get Your Coat – You've Pulled ISBN 1-85479-891-X

The Little Book of Crap Advice ISBN 1-85479883-9

The Little Book of Crap Excuses ISBN 1-85479-882-0

The Little Book of Totally Stupid Men ISBN 1-85479-833-2

The Little Couch Potato Book ISBN 1-85479-834-0

Welcome to Dumpsville ISBN 1-85479-880-4

Postage and packing outside the UK:
Europe: add 20% of retail price
Rest of the world: add 30% of retail price

To order any Michael O'Mara book please call our
credit-card hotline: **020 8324 5652**

Michael O'Mara Bookshop, BVCD
32–34 Park Royal Road, London NW10 7LN